# COWBOY'S
# NIGHT
# BEFORE
# CHRISTMAS

# COWBOY'S NIGHT BEFORE CHRISTMAS

Text
**Waddie Mitchell**

Illustration
**Don Weller**

GIBBS·SMITH
➜P
PUBLISHER

PEREGRINE SMITH BOOKS
SALT LAKE CITY

ISBN 0-87905-486-7
prpk 10: 0-87905-542-1
prpk 20: 0-87905-528-6
This is a Peregrine Smith
book, published by
Gibbs Smith, Publisher
P.O. Box 667
Layton, Utah 84041


95          5
Copyright ©  1992 by
Gibbs Smith, Publisher

'Twas
the night before
Christmas
and out
on the spread

We had finished
the chores
and was
goin' to bed.

'Tweren't much
Yule-tide spirit,
no stockin's
was hung,

No tree
was fixed up
and no carols
was sung.

'Fact,
none of the
cowboys
was sayin' a lot

As I tidied
the bedroll
that lay
on my cot.

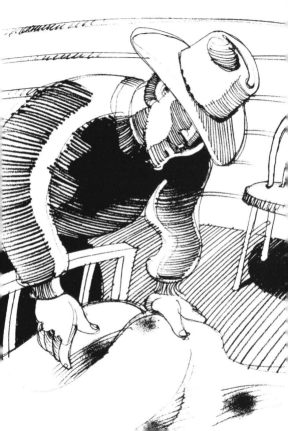

Been nearly
three weeks
without sugar
or mail

Since the wind
blew in drifts
that had closed up
the trail,

Which meant
that we wouldn't
see Christmas
in town.

An' I was fixin'
to lay
my ol' weary
bones down.

When out
in the yard
we heard
hoofbeats
and traces

As strange looks
come over
the cowpunchers'
faces.

There was
strainin' of harness
an' the distinct
muted sound

Of steel runners
slidin'
over snow-
covered ground.

So I pulls
on my boots
and I quits
my warm bed

An' peers out
the window
to see
team an' sled.

Then I yells
to the boys,
"Best build
a fresh pot!

"We've a guest
who'll appreciate
a cup
of it hot."

I opens the door
and
in comes
from the night

A
pot-bellied man,
frosted whiskers
turned white.

He seem'd
in a hurry;
he never
once tarried

As he gave
each man
somethin'
from the sack that
he carried.

He drank down
his coffee
then headed
back out;

Took holt of
the lines,
give a hoop
and a shout,

"On Spic
and on Span,
on Tom
and on Jerry.

"Es Christmas
amigos.
Hope I help
make it merry."

So we all
yelled in unison
back from
the door,

"You have.
An' Merry Christmas
to you, too,
Señor."

With a wink
and a flash
he was gone
in the night,

But his
coming
made every
man's attitude
bright.

'Twas
a Christmas
I'll remember
every year
without fail,

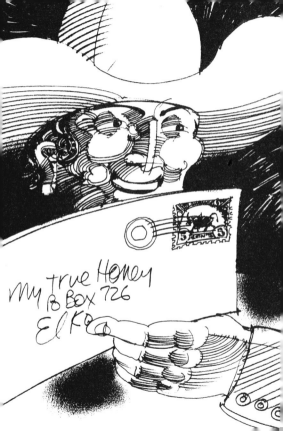

When *Santos*,
on contract,
got through
with the mail!